MEDITATIONS

"Set Your Affections on Things Above." Col.3:2

Patricia A. David

WestBow Press books may be ordered through booksellers or by contacting:

WestBow Press
A Division of Thomas Nelson & Zondervan
1663 Liberty Drive
Bloomington, IN 47403
www.westbowpress.com
1 (866) 928-1240

Author Photo for back cover taken by Kimberly David

Scripture taken from the King James Version of the Bible.

ISBN: 978-1-4908-1626-5 (sc)
ISBN: 978-1-4908-1627-2 (e)

Library of Congress Control Number: 2013921714

Printed in the United States of America.

WestBow Press rev. date: 1/16/2014

WESTBOW
PRESS
A DIVISION OF THOMAS NELSON
& ZONDERVAN

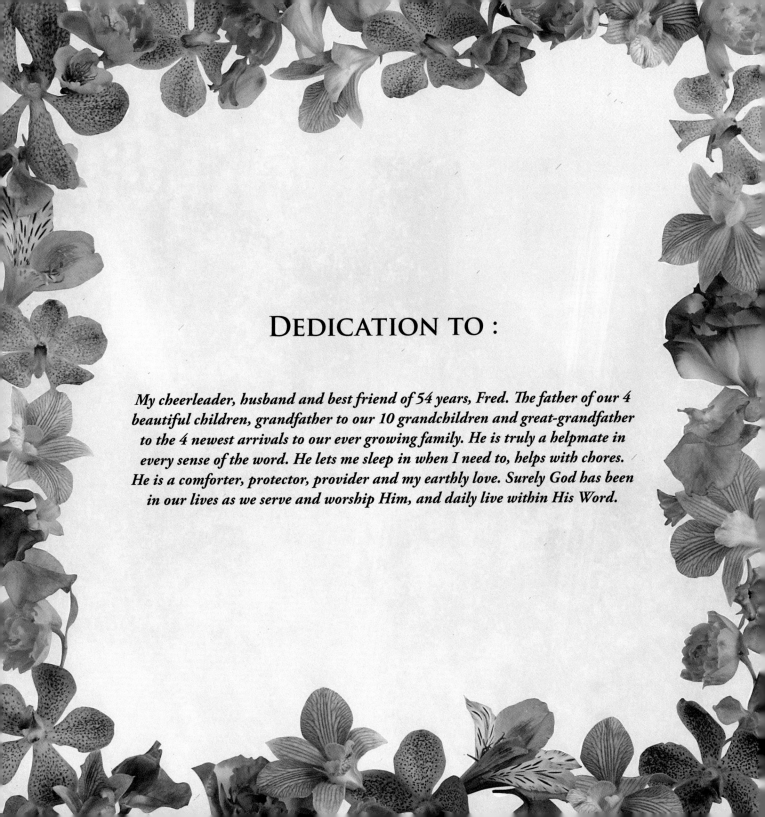

DEDICATION TO :

My cheerleader, husband and best friend of 54 years, Fred. The father of our 4 beautiful children, grandfather to our 10 grandchildren and great-grandfather to the 4 newest arrivals to our ever growing family. He is truly a helpmate in every sense of the word. He lets me sleep in when I need to, helps with chores. He is a comforter, protector, provider and my earthly love. Surely God has been in our lives as we serve and worship Him, and daily live within His Word.

HEAVEN OR HELL?

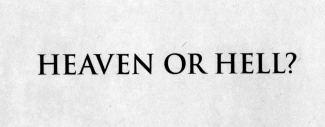

Up Calvary's Mountain Jesus climbed that day, for
sins He would pay. The wages of sin is death.
Do you come to Him and pray?
No, we curse and swear, and beat the air. We use drugs and try to
forget. In our heart we know we're not fit. Sexual pleasures have tied
us down, and yet we continue to be Hell bound. Cast your cares on
Jesus today. Don't let Satan lead you astray. Jesus paid for your debt of
sin, just repent an ask the Lord Jesus in. If you just walk away and say,
I will come to Him some other day. Boast not thyself of tomorrow.
For tomorrow you could be with Satan in sorrow. Don't put off what
must be done to dwell with Jesus, God's dear Son. When comes the
dawn, and He calls those who are sure and in Glory those will finally
be made pure.
3-29-2013

*"And I saw a new heaven and a new earth; for the first heaven and
the first earth were passed away; —
He that is unjust, let him be unjust still: and he
which filthy, let him be filthy still:"*
(Rev.21:1, 22:11)

BREATH OF LIFE

Breath of life so freely given,
From the Father up above.
Coming down to me in billows,
Lifts my soul in Heaven's Love.
For He makes my soul to hunger,
For the things of eternity.
Knowing I shall sing His praises
To the one who died to set me free.
Ring on eternal chorus,
He is worthy, He is worthy.
Ring on eternal chorus,
Sing praises to the Lord,
Sing praises to the Lord.

10-19-2001

"Make a joyful noise unto the Lord,
all ye lands. Serve the Lord with gladness: come
before his presence with singing.
Know ye that the Lord he is God: it is
he that hath made us, and not
we ourselves; we are his people, and the
sheep of his pastures, enter into his gates with
thanksgiving, and into his courts with
praise:be thankful unto him,
and bless his name."
(Ps. 100:1-4)

MAKE ME A MELODY

Make me a melody dear Lord,
To a soul without a song.
May I be a lighthouse on the shore.
To guide a traveler home.
Work through me Lord as only you can,
Bring these things to pass!
Knowing Lord that in Thee only,
this precious life will last.
Sept. 12, 1998

HELP ME LORD

Lift me up Lord, Lift me up Lord.
Help me stand, Please help me stand,
Held by your almighty hand.
In this land of endless night.
Let me see Your Glory Bright.
As a blind man longs for sight.
Lift me up Lord, Help me stand Lord,
Held by Your almighty hand.
Dec. 28, 2012

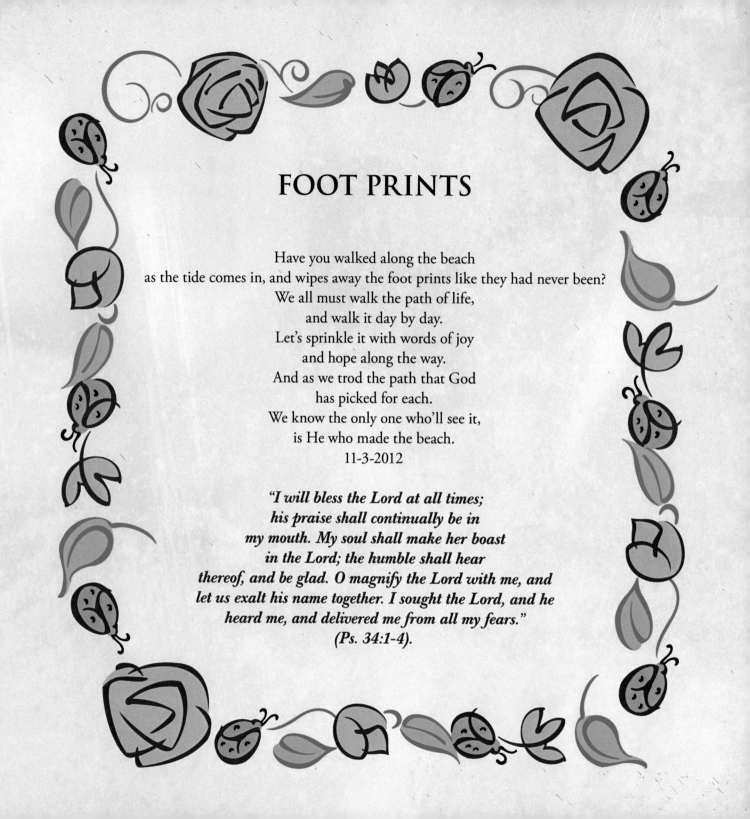

FOOT PRINTS

Have you walked along the beach
as the tide comes in, and wipes away the foot prints like they had never been?
We all must walk the path of life,
and walk it day by day.
Let's sprinkle it with words of joy
and hope along the way.
And as we trod the path that God
has picked for each.
We know the only one who'll see it,
is He who made the beach.
11-3-2012

*"I will bless the Lord at all times;
his praise shall continually be in
my mouth. My soul shall make her boast
in the Lord; the humble shall hear
thereof, and be glad. O magnify the Lord with me, and
let us exalt his name together. I sought the Lord, and he
heard me, and delivered me from all my fears."
(Ps. 34:1-4).*

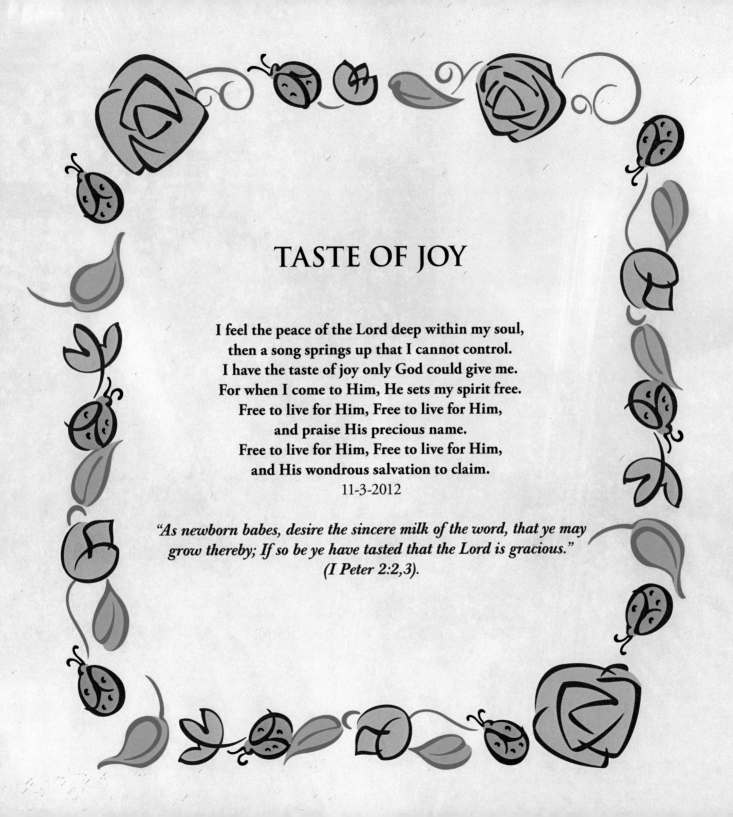

TASTE OF JOY

I feel the peace of the Lord deep within my soul,
then a song springs up that I cannot control.
I have the taste of joy only God could give me.
For when I come to Him, He sets my spirit free.
Free to live for Him, Free to live for Him,
and praise His precious name.
Free to live for Him, Free to live for Him,
and His wondrous salvation to claim.
11-3-2012

*"As newborn babes, desire the sincere milk of the word, that ye may
grow thereby; If so be ye have tasted that the Lord is gracious."*
(I Peter 2:2,3).

CARES TO ENDLESS PRAISE

When God hands you a broken heart,
do you handle it with care?
Do you draw from your
own wisdom as you
try to share?
The things we think
from within ourselves can
not be compared to those we receive
from God's Word, that with us He has shared. For God in Love wrote from above
to men His Spirit led, To guide
their thoughts and hands,
To write exactly what He said.
Throughout the ages that are past,
and ages yet to be,
We still can't fully see, The Father's Love to be.
But then one day, He'll open up our eyes
to endless praise, and we will dwell with Him
for endless days.
5-14-2013

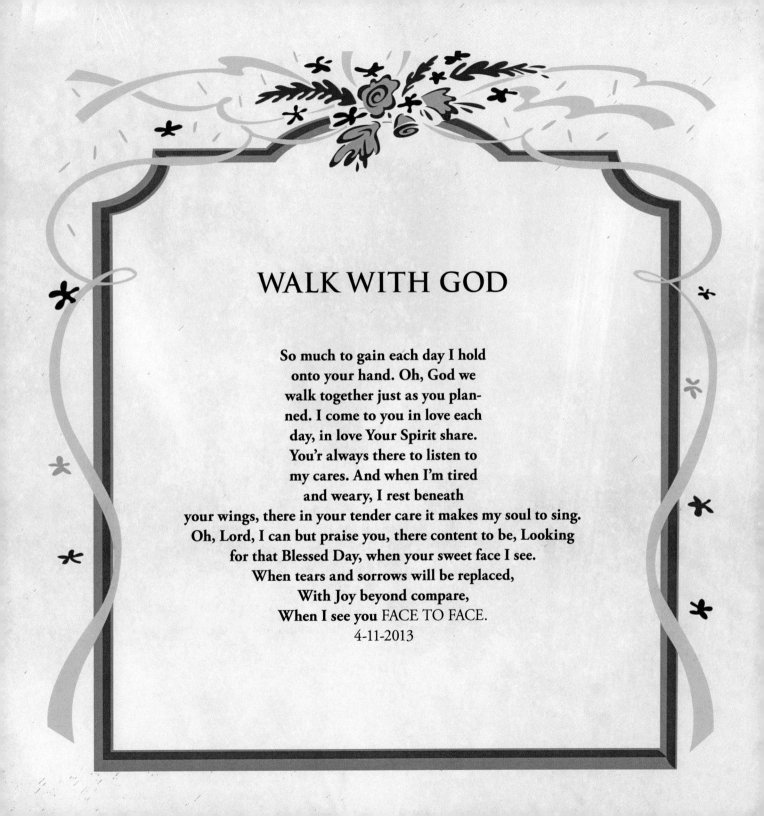

WALK WITH GOD

So much to gain each day I hold
onto your hand. Oh, God we
walk together just as you plan-
ned. I come to you in love each
day, in love Your Spirit share.
You'r always there to listen to
my cares. And when I'm tired
and weary, I rest beneath
your wings, there in your tender care it makes my soul to sing.
Oh, Lord, I can but praise you, there content to be, Looking
for that Blessed Day, when your sweet face I see.
When tears and sorrows will be replaced,
With Joy beyond compare,
When I see you FACE TO FACE.
4-11-2013

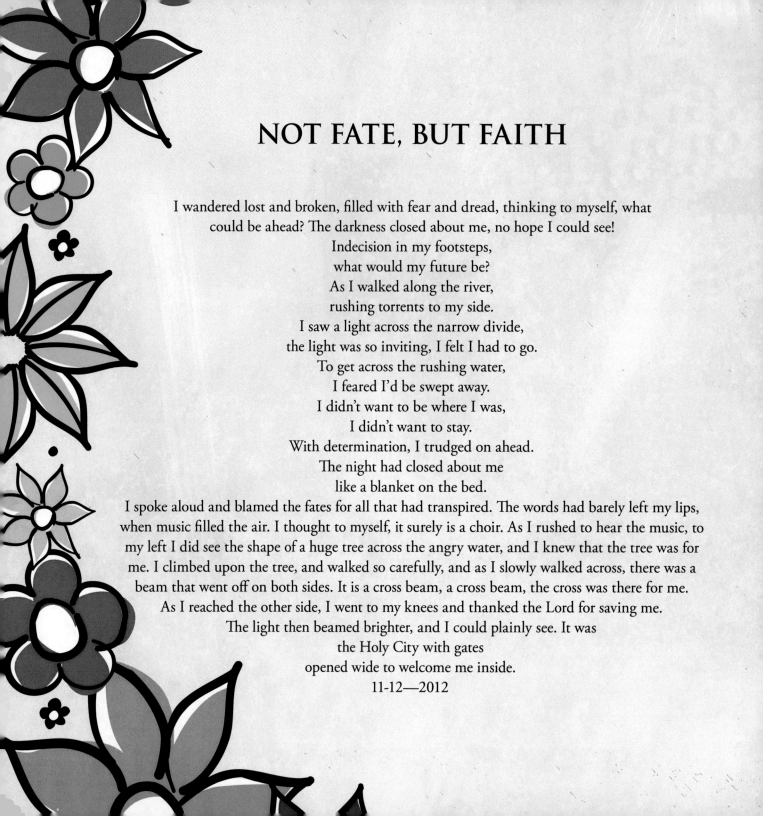

NOT FATE, BUT FAITH

I wandered lost and broken, filled with fear and dread, thinking to myself, what
could be ahead? The darkness closed about me, no hope I could see!
Indecision in my footsteps,
what would my future be?
As I walked along the river,
rushing torrents to my side.
I saw a light across the narrow divide,
the light was so inviting, I felt I had to go.
To get across the rushing water,
I feared I'd be swept away.
I didn't want to be where I was,
I didn't want to stay.
With determination, I trudged on ahead.
The night had closed about me
like a blanket on the bed.
I spoke aloud and blamed the fates for all that had transpired. The words had barely left my lips,
when music filled the air. I thought to myself, it surely is a choir. As I rushed to hear the music, to
my left I did see the shape of a huge tree across the angry water, and I knew that the tree was for
me. I climbed upon the tree, and walked so carefully, and as I slowly walked across, there was a
beam that went off on both sides. It is a cross beam, a cross beam, the cross was there for me.
As I reached the other side, I went to my knees and thanked the Lord for saving me.
The light then beamed brighter, and I could plainly see. It was
the Holy City with gates
opened wide to welcome me inside.
11-12—2012

SOMEDAY SOON

As I go from day to day, I hear of
Satan having his way.
Dealing with fear and dread, I feel I know that Satan is so real.
But as I reflect in my mind,
Against Christ's side, I recline.
His perfect rest He gives to me,
I sit contented at Jesus knee.
Let my steps be quick and sure. Not led away by earthly lure. Till someday
soon ,I see God's face. I'll repeat again an again,"saved by grace."
For then there'll be no fear or doubt.
And, with the saints, we will
stand and shout.
For in His presence we will be,
forever together for all eternity.
Father remind us each day we're here,
Let our ears be tuned to hear.
The still small voice each has inside,
That in You alone, we can truly abide.

11-11-2012

"If ye then be risen with Christ,
seek those things which are above; where Christ sitteth on the right hand
of God. Set your affection on things above, not on things on the earth.
For ye are dead, and your life is hid with Christ in God."
(Col. 3:1-3)

WHAT A DAY!

**One day in Heaven our new life will begin. One day in heaven
we'll be free from from all sin. Shouting and praising
evermore to begin.**

Oh, what a wonderful day!
Look can you see Him,
the Lord on His throne.
There as He welcomes each one of us Home. Crying is ended, tears wiped away,
Oh, what a wonderful day!
Seeing our loved ones
who have gone on before.
Those who now greet us
on Heaven's bright shore. There we will be gathered for evermore.
Oh, what a wonderful Day!
Now, we are waiting that Glorious Day,
When all our burdens will be taken away.
Be faithful my friends,
it won't be long. Christ will
replace our crying, with a song.
Oh, what a wonderful Day!
(4-16-2013)

HE REACHED OUT

As the mountains reach towards the sky,
And the eagle stretches his wings to fly.
The streams run downward to a
beautiful fall.
It splashes over the rocks below,
and spreads it's water where it needs to go.
The trees, flowers, animals and bird,
drink from its flow.
Then downwards, downward,
downward it goes.
God causes the courses of lands and seas,
and the planets to move in their paths
across the sky, and yet
He has time for you an I.
And yet with all that God has to do,
He planned salvation for me and you.
He sent His Son Jesus to die in our place,
to take away our sins,
and showered us with grace.
And at your hearts, He's knocking today.
So, please, please, please
don't turn Him away!
NOW IS THE DAY OF SALVATION.
(June 9, 2006)

"Jesus saith unto her, I am the resurrection and the life; he that believeth in me, though he were dead, yet shall he live; And whosoever liveth and believeth in me shall never die. Believest thou this?"
(John 11:25,26)

TO GOD BE THE GLORY

In the stillness of the Morning,
my thoughts are drawn to You. Oh, creator of the universe, Your
ways are bright and true. In time and space, You made a place
for sun and moon to shine.
And put each star across the span, like diamonds in the sky.
And as I looked for you
Dear Lord, You had a plan for me. You took me by my heart,
and led me to Calvary To show me there of Your great Love,
brought down to set me free.
For not by works of goodness will your blessed face I see. But only
by your Precious Blood, that you shed that day for me.
Let me not rest in my best,
or think that it is me.
But, let me rest upon your breast
and know it is of thee.
(3-25-2013)

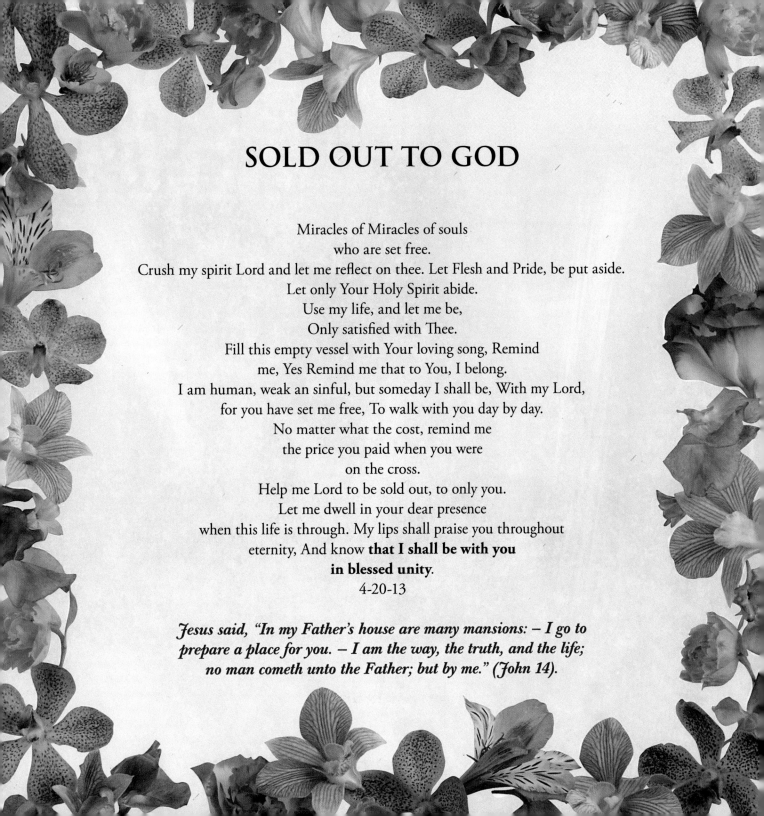

SOLD OUT TO GOD

Miracles of Miracles of souls
who are set free.
Crush my spirit Lord and let me reflect on thee. Let Flesh and Pride, be put aside.
Let only Your Holy Spirit abide.
Use my life, and let me be,
Only satisfied with Thee.
Fill this empty vessel with Your loving song, Remind
me, Yes Remind me that to You, I belong.
I am human, weak an sinful, but someday I shall be, With my Lord,
for you have set me free, To walk with you day by day.
No matter what the cost, remind me
the price you paid when you were
on the cross.
Help me Lord to be sold out, to only you.
Let me dwell in your dear presence
when this life is through. My lips shall praise you throughout
eternity, And know **that I shall be with you
in blessed unity**.
4-20-13

*Jesus said, "In my Father's house are many mansions: — I go to
prepare a place for you. — I am the way, the truth, and the life;
no man cometh unto the Father; but by me." (John 14).*

SWEET REFRAIN

Sing me that song again.
That perfect melody, that lifts my soul in praise, To have Jesus Christ in my days.
It puts my soul to rest, Because He is the very best. It's message clear
and plain, Became my sweet refrain. When Jesus died for me, My
soul He did set free. Way back on Calvary's tree He paid the sin debt
for me. So sing that song once again, I love to hear it more.
Let nations memorize the score.
The message is complete, So then repeat and repeat, Till
Jesus sweeps us off our feet, On that glad day
When God calls us away.
4-8-2013

QUIET PEACE

As the snowflakes settle softly to the earth,
To decorate the land around and give it renewed worth. So in faith I
come to God in the quietness of my soul, And become more thankful
of the truth, that Jesus made me whole. The beauty of its brightness,
To make me clean and look so white. I ask Jesus to forgive
me and take away my sin, And
let His Holy Spirit come and dwell
within. And now I am ready
to meet my Lord someday.
I wait for Him to call me,
to go with Him and stay.
3-25-2013

REUNION DAY
To the tune: ROCK OF AGES

Trumpets sounding in the streets
Angels praising in the squares
Praising GOD in songs so sweet
Excitement fills the air,
Declaring we are finally home,
Cast our crown before HIS throne
Amazing grace how sweet the sound,
Which in Heaven now abounds,
Tears of sadness wiped away,
It's the great Reunion day,
Saints now dressed in robes of white
Oh, to see this, blessed sight
Now encourage one and all,
Listen for the Spirit's call
Do not tarry in the way
You could miss it if you stray,
Be prepared with lamp all trimmed,
When it's time to enter in.
Rock of ages, cleft for me,
Let me hide myself in Thee
Jan. 29, 2010

GOD'S BIGGER THAN MY PLANS

"Being confident
of this very thing, that he which hath begun
a good work in you will perform it until
the day of Jesus Christ."
(Phil. 1:6).

As time goes by, we get older.
But, God's Word is fresh and must be told.
We are partners with those who've gone before.
And, we trust in Jesus to open the door. Let
God's Word explode out of our life. Tearing
down the stronghold of Satan's strife. So
whether in prison, or on a tropic isle, continue,
yes, continue to push on with a smile.
God has a reason for each thing He allows,
whether we are driving or pushing a plow.
Trust God's leading each and every mile. Count
it all joy, no matter the cost. Let Christ be your
guide to win the lost. For Satan wants to send
us on a down hill slide. But, in the Lord,
we can safely abide. Tell it, and show it
each step you take.
We don't do it for us, but our Lord's sake.
(6-23-2013)

"– Christ in you, the hope of glory: Whom
we preach, warning every man, teaching
every man in all wisdom; that we may
present every man perfect in Christ Jesus."
(Col. 1:27, 28)

"As ye have therefore received Christ Jesus the Lord,
so walk ye in him: Rooted and built up in him, and
stabiles in the faith, as ye have taught, abounding therein with
thanksgiving. –
For in him dwelleth all the fullness of the Godhead bodily.
And ye are complete in him, which is the
head of all principality and power:"
(Col. 2:6,7, 9,10)

"If ye be risen with Christ, seek those things which are above;
where Christ sitteth on the right hand of God.
Set your affection on things above, not on things on the earth."
(Col. 3:1,2)

HIS ABILITY

Nothing in this life I find can truly satisfy.
For all the things around
have slowly passed away.
But as I stumble through this life
of worry and despair,
I found a light that shown so bright,
from someone who really cared.
I found the person Jesus, the mighty
Son of God, Who died for me, and
set me free from sins I have within.
For all are born in sin you know,
and all our lives do show it.
All we have to do is come to God.
Do it this very day. Ask Christ in
to forgive your sin. He will make you
new within. Talk to Him each day,
as you come to pray. Make Him Lord
of all, or He's not Lord at all.
Living a Christian life is
not your responsibility,
It's your response
to His ability..
3-4-2013

THE PRECIOUS ONE

How was it that I heard of Christ?
Was it through words of someone's views?
Something that could change my life anew? Did it challenge my very soul,
And lead me to the Lord's control?
So now do I change and place my thoughts in other ways?
Do I have a better plan each day,
rather then in Thee, my Lord to stay?
Not in my ways that I have planned,
But in your works alone I stand.
On Christ the solid Rock I stand,
All other ground is sinking sand.
So when I come to you each day,
I know you see my life, and where I stay.
No one could guide me as you do.
For only in you all truth is new.
And only as Your truth is known,
We will arrive before your throne.
Only as we trust in Christ's blood alone.
Praise you God, for all you've done.
By sending us Your Precious Son.

(6-21-2013)

GO SCRUB THAT

Are we infected by the world?
Or the protection of God's sword?
Pure Spiritual milk from God's Word we crave, and turn away
from Satan's sludge, he gave.
And when we give, can we out give the Lord, who gave His all our
souls to reclaim. And make us equal in Him the same. Let God's
word scrub us day by day, and in God's healing we will stay.
So in God's praise each day we abide.
And we know the difference between
God's better and best,
as we walk by Jesus side.
So change us Lord, give us your mind.
And lead us to those who are still blind.
Instill in us a spirit to win the lost.
And remember always the
price of you're cross. (6-21-2013)

"When I call to remembrance the unfeigned faith that is thee, which dwelt first in thy grandmother Lois, and thy mother Eunice; and I am persuaded that in thee also."
(II Tim.1:5).
"Wherefore laying aside all malice, and all guile, and hypocrisies, and envies, and all evil speaking, As newborn babes, desire the sincere milk of the word, that ye may grow thereby:" (I Peter 2:1,2).
"For ye know the grace of our Lord Jesus Christ, that, though he was rich, yet for your your sakes he became poor, that ye through his poverty might be rich." (II Cor. 8:9).
"And God is able to make all grace abound towards you; that ye always having all sufficiency in all things, may abound to every good work." (II Cor. 9:8).

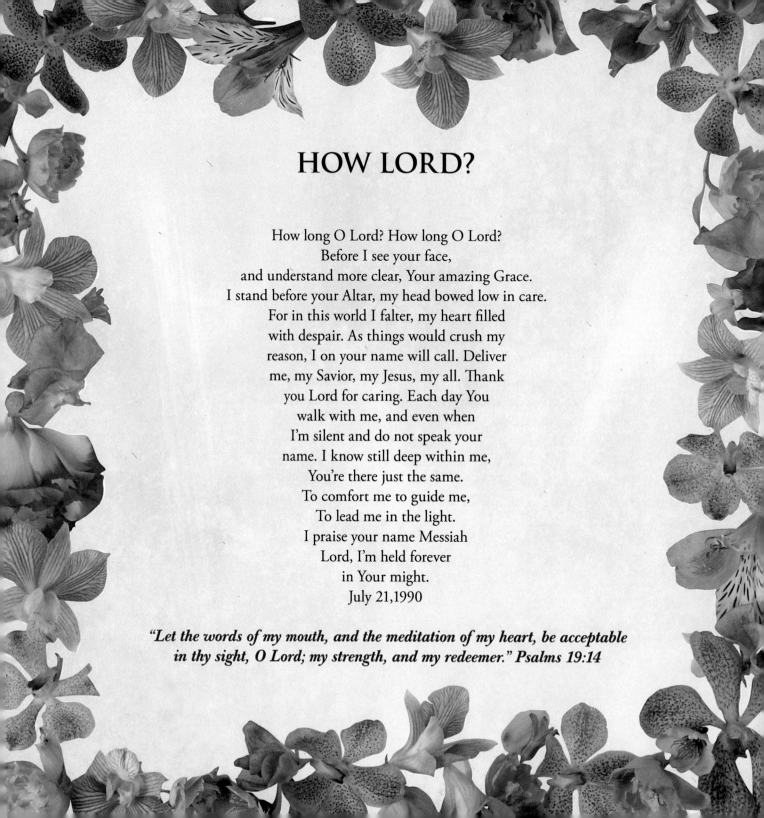

HOW LORD?

How long O Lord? How long O Lord?
Before I see your face,
and understand more clear, Your amazing Grace.
I stand before your Altar, my head bowed low in care.
For in this world I falter, my heart filled
with despair. As things would crush my
reason, I on your name will call. Deliver
me, my Savior, my Jesus, my all. Thank
you Lord for caring. Each day You
walk with me, and even when
I'm silent and do not speak your
name. I know still deep within me,
You're there just the same.
To comfort me to guide me,
To lead me in the light.
I praise your name Messiah
Lord, I'm held forever
in Your might.
July 21,1990

"Let the words of my mouth, and the meditation of my heart, be acceptable
in thy sight, O Lord; my strength, and my redeemer." Psalms 19:14

FATHER OF LIES

Oh, what a tangled web we weave,
when first we practice to deceive.
One lie upon another told,
till each time they get more bold.
Lies are such a slippery slope, Once
caught, we slide without much hope.
Then the lies begin to grow,
Be-it even ever so slow.
Bigger and bigger the truth we bend,
Then we come to an awful end.
Because, it was Satan that taught
us first, To look good to others
we did thirst. Now they tumble off
our tongue, without a thought, like
we were young. We've believed
the unholy one, And he just laughs
at us in fun. For once a lie has once
begun, It's never finished, it's never done.
But then if the truth be ever said,
It's on God's list of ours to be read.
Think, Oh think before you speak,
Who might read
your words next week!
(10-21-2010)

ARRIVAL AT HOME

I am a prisoner of the Lord,
Walking with Him is my reward.
Safely through this life He guides my path.
Then to arrive at home at last.
Our hope is only in our King,
In Him our hearts can gladly sing.
Praises each day His presence bring.
There like the eagle, we take flight.
Soaring upward much higher than the heights.
Peace and safety to ever be,
Free from life's trial for all eternity!
(6-20-13)

GOD'S WORKS

Joy and contentment
God has given me,
For when I go to Him each day,
my burdens there I leave.
Such peace and comfort,
God shines upon my soul.
That I might understand
Your Words, and be made whole.
In praise my heart ascends to
heights unknown.
Looking for that blessed day
around your throne.
(6-20-2013)

TRUST AND OBEY

When Satan causes my heart to fear and whispers in my ear,
What I want is doomed to fail, and will take a million years.
I stand and tell him he is a liar and has been from the start,
When with pride he lifted himself and darkened his heart.
For when we trust within ourselves we can only fail,
for on our own we are to frail.
But when we look to Christ, repent an ask HIM to abide
and never trust our own strength but walk by JESUS' side.
In GOD we have more strength then we could ever measure,
For CHRIST alone is our treasure of treasures.
So cling to CHRIST and read HIS word, and in HIS truth we stay
remember, yes remember to look to HIM and pray
10/12/13

*"That ye might walk worthy of the Lord unto all pleasing, being fruitful
in every good work, And increasing in the knowledge of God."
(Colossians 1:10)*

HIGH AND LIFTED UP

I call myself to look inside,
to see where my soul does abide.
To make a check list of hurts today,
or consider what I want to repay.
Do I believe I'm always right,
Therefore it's by my might.
Or, should I strive for unity,
Or push the things that I believe. Let me Lord draw close to you,
My friend who's pure
and true. Teach me your
humility, that you
humbled yourself to the
death on the tree. So
let me live not for me
alone, but worship you
upon your throne. Clear
my path from day to day,
Keep my heart in your right way. For when the road is bright
an clear, It's only Lord because You are near.
When I would hold others in disgrace,
Let me hold the mirror to my face.
For you see me when I try to hide,
And for all my sins,
You bled and died.
For You are Holy above all,
And still You wait for our weak call.
Christ is with you wherever you go,
So call on Him, and don't be slow.
(5-12-2013)

"Study to shew thyself approved unto God,
a workman that neediest not be ashamed,
rightly dividing the word of truth."
(2 Tim. 2:15)

"Finally, brethren,
whatsoever things are true,
whatsoever things are honest,
whatsoever things are just,
whatsoever things are pure,
whatsoever things are lovely,
whatsoever things are of
good report;
if there be any virtue, and if there be any praise,
think on these things."
(Philippians 4;8)

HIS GENTLE VOICE

When days are lonely and drear,
My fears seem to appear.
Hope had turned it's back on me,
What in life was left to see.
Then I cried out in despair,
Doesn't anybody really care?
That is when His Gentile Voice
came in. He whispered so sweet,
I died to make your life complete.
I came to take away your sins.
You simply asked me to come in.
Now, there's joy beyond compare.
I can see Him everywhere.
And I remember when
His Gentle voice came in,
When my new life did begin!
(9-24-2010)

THE ROAD TO EMMAUS

He is not here, He is risen as He said.
He is risen, He is risen, praise the Lord.
Let us share in the joy of our blessed Lord.
Rejoice in His love, in spite of
the slowness of our hearts.
Stay with us LORD, and thy wisdom to import. Where lies
our hopes an our desire, we work, we study for all
we aspire. Our hopes, our dreams
should be in Christ, and let Him
guide our way. He came, He shared,
He died for us that day.
Why seek ye the living among
the dead? He is not here,
HE HAS RISEN AS HE SAID.
(January 27, 2013)

GUIDANCE

Direct me Lord as I enter a
new day. Lead me to the needy,
and touch my heart to pray.
Let me not draw upon wisdom
of my own.
But early in each day
seek wisdom from your throne.
Guide my footsteps,
as on your Spirit I call.
May I not overlook anyone
big or small.
Let me show the grace of God
upon my face.
Let my words spring forth,
with your Divine grace.
When the hurting I encounter,
let me not turn aside,
Keep me sensitive to the feelings
they harbor inside.

For my life is blest
by your words,
as I travel day by day.
Hosannas let my praises be,
as I walk in your way.
And if this be my last day,
let me not balk.
May I not just talk the talk,
but walk the walk.
Dec. 28, 2012

*"He that spared not his
own son, but delivered him up
for us all, how shall he not
with him also freely give us
all things?"*
(Rom. 8:32)

LOOK AND SEE

Climb up Calvary's Mountain. Look around, For all you can see.
Can you picture our Savior Jesus, as He died for you and me. Christ was
on a Mission from His Father up above. Taking our burdens, dying for us
in love. When I think of all Christ did for me, As he hung on Calvary's
tree, I will praise Him all day long. For Christ has given me a song.
(Dec. 28, 2010)

LISTEN CAREFULLY

Precious are your precepts to guide us day by day. When we need answers
to our questions, You remind us to pray. No matter what the struggle may
be, We can trust Jesus, and wait to see. How He works it out each day,
No matter, come what may.
Peace and joy, He gives to all
Who in His precious name do call.
(Nov. 23, 2012)

GOD HOLDS OUR TOMORROW

Laugh out loud, to feel free within. To know that you
are free from sin. Let your heart leap for joy.
No longer Satan's toy. Catch a glimpse of heaven view. Made for me and made for you.
Be comforted in your soul, For God has made you whole. So laugh out loud once again,
Turn to Satan with a grin. For God holds your destiny For all eternity.
Feb. 27, 2013

Never More to Roam

Yesterday I dreamed a dream that swept my soul with joy,
I saw a land where milk and honey flowed all life
was free from pain and care,
An as I took a deep breath the scent of flowers filled the air.
Children running here and there, laughter filled my heart
an I felt that I would shout,
For at last my soul was free for JESUS had lifted me out.
My back was straightened, legs and body strong,
GOD has placed within me a new song.
For GOD had drawn me to HIMSELF never more to roam.
Now with the millions of others we sing praises around GOD'S throne
Smiling faces greet me and praises filled the air,
but I wonder, as I wander upon the earth I roam,
will I see your face when I get home?
10/14/13

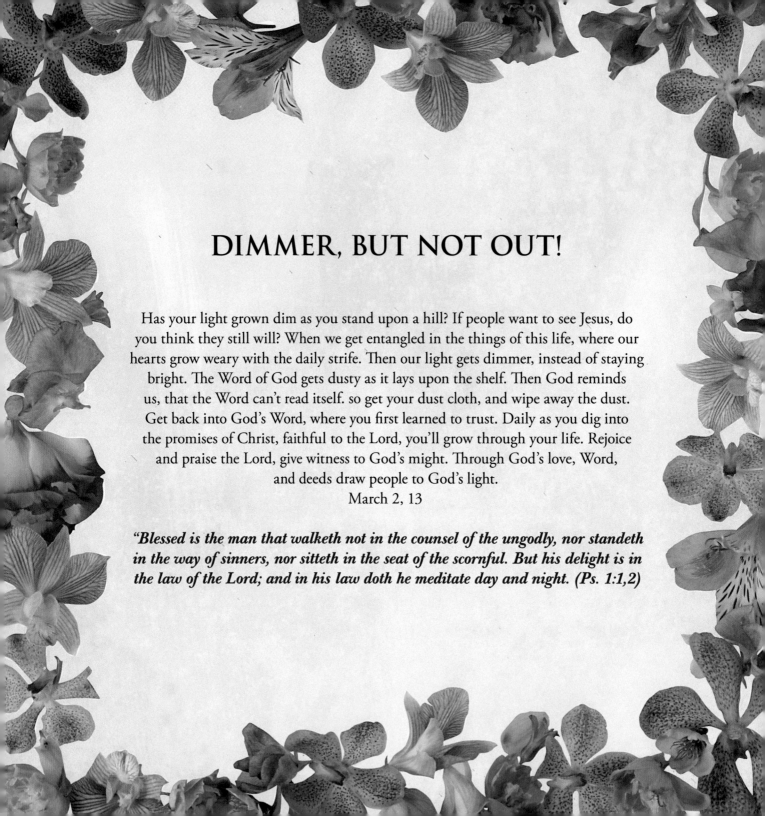

DIMMER, BUT NOT OUT!

Has your light grown dim as you stand upon a hill? If people want to see Jesus, do you think they still will? When we get entangled in the things of this life, where our hearts grow weary with the daily strife. Then our light gets dimmer, instead of staying bright. The Word of God gets dusty as it lays upon the shelf. Then God reminds us, that the Word can't read itself. so get your dust cloth, and wipe away the dust. Get back into God's Word, where you first learned to trust. Daily as you dig into the promises of Christ, faithful to the Lord, you'll grow through your life. Rejoice and praise the Lord, give witness to God's might. Through God's love, Word, and deeds draw people to God's light.

March 2, 13

"Blessed is the man that walketh not in the counsel of the ungodly, nor standeth in the way of sinners, nor sitteth in the seat of the scornful. But his delight is in the law of the Lord; and in his law doth he meditate day and night. (Ps. 1:1,2)

WHITE LIES?

A lie is a lie no matter how small,
and they come back to haunt you all,
For once a lie has begun,
it grows and grows it's never done.
A lie will demand you dress it more,
Then one day it will come to your door.
When you are caught in a lie the matter is bad,
for you can lose the friendships you once had.
Trust has been broken walls are torn down,
you feel like living in another town.
The Bible quotes let your words be true,
so each one you talk to can believe in you.
In Matthew 5:37, "let your yea, be yea and your nay, be nay"
what more does GOD have to say?
10/20/13

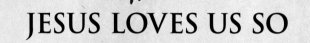

JESUS LOVES US SO

Do you know Him,
the one who died for you?
Did you trust Him,
To make your life anew?
Will you share Him,
With those who do not know?
Can you tell them that
Jesus loves them so?
Can you witness to those Lost in sin?
Will you tell them that they
can be cleansed within?
Do you care for those, You see each day?
Do not turn your back and walk away.
They may not Know the way to Heaven's door. Can you share that Jesus
Loves them more. Can you praise Him, each and everyday? Do you listen,
every time you pray? Make sure to let Him lead you all the way. Be ready to
go with Him One glorious day. Still tell them that Jesus loves them so.
(April 30-2013)

"Behold, what manner of love
the Father hath bestowed upon us, that we should be called the sons of God;
therefore the world knoweth us not, because it knew him not. Beloved, now
are we the sons of God, and it doth not appear what we shall be; but we
know that, when he shall appear, we shall be like him;—" (I John 3:1,2).

SOFTLY HE COMES

Gently He wakes me in the still of the morn. Sweetly He reminds me, the reason He was born. Again He reminds me, before my eyes could see, He had planned my life out, and what I was meant to be. Softly He touches me and whispers in my ear, that His presence goes before me, and He is always near. I know when I reach out to Him, He's always reaching back. So in His joy, and love and hope, I shall never lack. He keeps me graciously each day, upheld by strong hands. Quietly He reminds me of a home prepared for me in His eternal land. Thank you Lord for loving me, and teaching me to smile. For showing me that you have been there all the while. From eternity past, to eternity future, my life will ever be, Covered by your presence, for all eternity. (Nov. 23, 2012).

"Through God we shall do valiantly:
for he it is that shall tread down
our enemies." Ps.60:12.

THE TRUTH, TO GOOD TO BE TRUE!

Scared of shadows, afraid of all,
We can blame it on the fall.
When Adam and Eve disobeyed
and sinned, Inviting Satan to come in.
From age to age it remains the same,
Satan continues to plan his games.
Lying, cheating, blaming, desires,
Wanting more and more to acquire.
God comes to earth as a new born babe.
His lowly birth in a manger laid.
A place to rest His weary head.
At the age of 12, He amazed the Scribes.
For He knew all the sages, and watched their lives. Jesus knew from eternity past.
He alone had the answer of sin at last.
The way He chose to redeem us was hard,
But then again no one else was the Lord.

He died on the cross to redeem mankind,
To turn from sin, those who are blind.
Three days He stayed within the grave,
Then arose for us, new life He gave.
He did all this for you and me,
To set our condemned souls free.
Accept Him, repent, and ask Him in.
And He alone can take away your sin.
Then thank Him, and praise Him,
your soul set free.
I'll praise Him too,
He did the same thing for me.
Feb. 27, 2013

*"I am crucified with Christ:
nevertheless
I, live; yet not I, but
Christ liveth in me:"
(Gal. 2:20)*

IT WON'T BE LONG

It won't be long now, Till
the face of Christ we will see.
It won't be long now, Till He comes for you and me.
It won't be long now, Till we see Him in the air, It won't be long now, Till eternal
peace we share. It won't be long now, Till we are with our King. It won't be long now,
Till we will shout and sing Heaven is a wonderful place, I want to see my Savior's face.
Jan. 6, 2013

AMAZED

Continually I stand amazed
at the Light showered from above.
Beneath it's glow, I bask,
I know in God's surrounding love,
I cannot tell from day to day,
which way my feet will go.
But this I know, and this I'll tell,
That Jesus loves me so.
July 21, 1990

OH, WHAT JOY!

Lift up your voice to the
King of all ages.
Shout for the joy that's in your heart.
Pray for the ones who haven't
heard the blessed story.
How Christ came down
to redeem us and take us to Glory.
Put a smile on your face for the whole human race. Share the message
with all who will hear. Lift your voice and sing to our eternal King.
Come before His throne in worship everyday. Never fear, never doubt,
only cheer and shout.
For our eternal **path is clear,**
Draw close to Jesus
and stay near.
Jan. 6, 2013

"Blessed is the man that walk—eth not in the counsel of the un—godly, nor standeth in the way of sinners, nor sitteth in the seat of scornful. But his delight is in the law of the Lord; and in his law doth he meditate day and night. And he shall be like a tree plant—ed by the rivers of water, that bring forth his fruit in his season; his leaf also shall not wither; and whatsoever he doeth shall pros—per. The ungodly are not so: but are like the chaff which the wind driveth away. Therefore the ungodly shall not stand in the judgment, nor sinners in the congregation of the righteous. For the Lord knoweth the way of the righteous: but the way of the un—godly shall perish." (Psalms 1).

WANDERING

It's an uphill battle you hear folks say.
They Grumble and groan all day.
They gripe and they moan
to be left alone.

But if the truth be told,
Their heart is hard and cold.
In the valley of life they wander
Never thinking of the life they've squandered.

Till one day in a mirror they spy
The deadness in their eyes.
A face whose soul longs for grace,
Starts to look for the Saviour's face.
They find that God's been waiting
all the time, To change their life
from dead to subline. And to lift
their spirit up in time. As you
look around you at the crowd
today. Is their someone's spirit
you could lift along the way.
Jesus now entreat us to
share His Bless Good News.

**Win them to Jesus,
and Satan will lose.**
(2-27-2013)

LIKE MINDED

God takes the simple and the weak,
To confound the noble an unique.
God gives us wisdom beyond our years,
And helps us to be like-minded and clear,
In our weakness we are made whole,
In our Simple minds,
He gives answers to our Souls.
10-24-2010

*"Mine eyes prevent the night
watches, that I might
meditate in thy word."*
Psalms 119:148

RENEWED

Make me a melody dear Lord,
To a soul without a song.
May I be a lighthouse on the shore,
To guide a weary traveler home.
Work through me Lord as only you can,
bring all these things from your
Word to pass.
Knowing Lord that in thee only,
This precious life will last.
10-19-2001

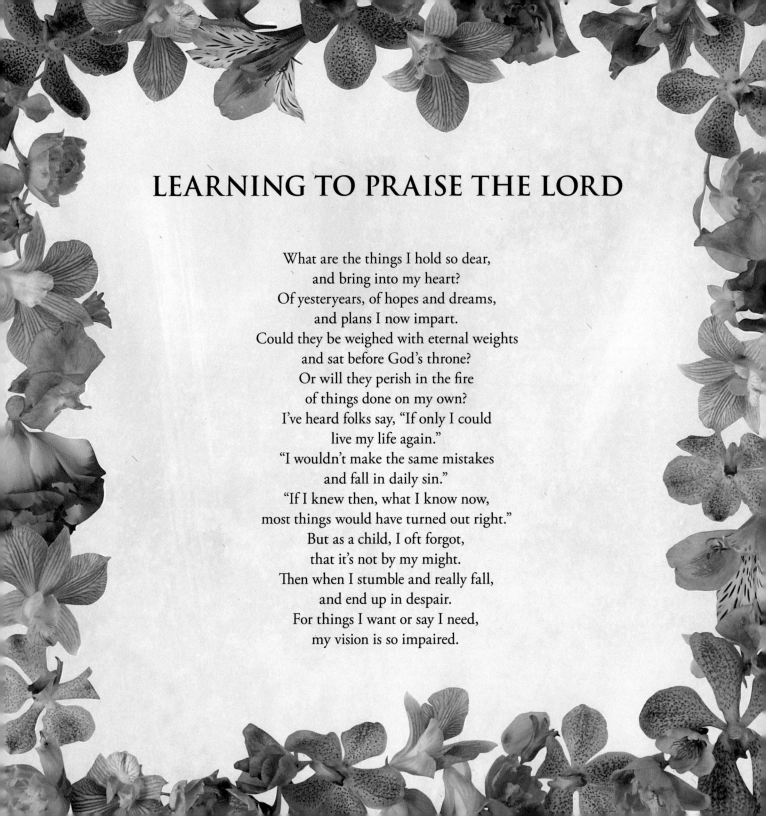

LEARNING TO PRAISE THE LORD

What are the things I hold so dear,
and bring into my heart?
Of yesteryears, of hopes and dreams,
and plans I now impart.
Could they be weighed with eternal weights
and sat before God's throne?
Or will they perish in the fire
of things done on my own?
I've heard folks say, "If only I could
live my life again."
"I wouldn't make the same mistakes
and fall in daily sin."
"If I knew then, what I know now,
most things would have turned out right."
But as a child, I oft forgot,
that it's not by my might.
Then when I stumble and really fall,
and end up in despair.
For things I want or say I need,
my vision is so impaired.

It's by God's grace, and by His Love,
That drew me to His side.
Then to my life, my heart, my soul,
His blood He did apply.
So praise the Lord and seek His face,
and live within His Grace.
He is the one who lifts me up,
who sets my feet aright.
He is the One who gives a song,
to see me through the night.
Lord lift me up and guide me on,
to your eternal shore.
Cause me to seek your loving face,
more and more and more.
May 1990

"Open thou mine eyes, that I may
behold wondrous things out
of thy law."
Psalms 119:18

GOD'S WILL

A farmer
was walking
to town leading a cow,
as he passed another farmer seated
on his porch. The farmer called out, "Where are you going my friend? The farmer
with the cow replied, "I'm going to town to sell my cow." The man on the porch
said, Don't you mean if the Lord wills it, you are going to town to sell the cow?
The man with the cow, "No, I mean I'm going to town to sell my cow."
Then he walked on toward town. About ten minutes later, the man
came walking back without his cow. His friend knew that he hadn't
had time to get to town, so he asked, "What happened?"
The man told him, "As he was walking,
a bolt of lightning hit the cow
and killed it."
"Well", said the man on the porch,
"What are you going to do now?"
"I'm going home." And he started off.
Then he turns and came back and
said, "I mean if it's the Lord's will,
I'm going home."
9-28-2002

GLAD DAY

I have a new song to sing,
For Jesus is my king.
For He heard my plea,
And set my poor soul free.
And when He comes at last,
Or, when this poor life is past.
There will be life without end, In the presence of my dear
friend, Jesus Christ, the one who loves me so.
Praise and Glory will resound,
For in God's Love that does abound.
all God's children gathered round
On that Glad day.
(March 11, 2013)

*"And God shall wipe away all tears from their eyes; and there shall
be no more death, neither sorrow, nor crying, neither shall be any
more pain; for the former things are passed away." (Rev. 21:4).*

WAITING ON GOD

SONG

The faster I go, the behinder I get,
When traveling along life's busy highways.
The faster I go, the behinder I get,
When I try to do it my own way.

CHORUS: Each day seems to bring me
it's Pascal of sorrow
Each day seems to bring me
no hope for tomorrow.

Until I met the Lord
and gave Him all of my cares
and let Him share with me
His death on Calvary.

The farther I go with the Lord each day
I know His provisions will keep me
Much farther I go with the Lord each day
When I pray to do it God's own way
When I pray to do it God's own way.
7-10-1974

"Let not your heart be troubled; ye believe
in God, believe also in me. In my Father's house
are many mansions; if it were not so,
I would have told you. I go to prepare
a place for you. And if I go and prepare a place for you, I will come
again, and receive you unto myself; that where I am, there ye may
be also. — Jesus saith unto him, I am the way, the truth, and the
life; no man cometh unto cometh unto the Father; but by me."
John 14:1-6

HE LOVED ME FIRST

He sought me when no one else
would look my way,
He picked me up when my path
had gone astray.
He carried me along the
rough and winding roads,
I could feel His presence,
helping with each heavy load.
He loved me before I knew I needed love,
and guides me gently
by His Words from above.
He convicts me when I chose to
ignore His voice,
But loves me even when
I make the wrong choice.
He loved me first and the very best,
Father help me to love
you with my very best.
8-23-99

*"Cause me to hear thy loving
kindness in the morning;
for in the do I trust; cause
me to know the way
wherein I should walk;
for I lift up my soul unto
thee. Deliver me, O Lord,
from mine enemies: I flee
unto thee to hide me."*
Psalms 143:8,9

ACCOUNTABLE TO GOD

Close accounts with God.
We pray for day by day.
Be up to date and peace within.
Desire to be freed from all sin.

In Awe of you, I come today,
Seek your presence, there to stay.
May joy leap to my lips,
open them wide,
Lord as you walk with me
side by side.

You hold me up and help me stand,
My steps are guided in you hands.
So lead me straight toward
your throne,
And remind me often of
our Heavenly home.

Walk beside me day by day,
Hear my thoughts as I pray.
Grant me strength to face
sorrow and pain.
Help me show others of Heaven
to gain. A heart of love, I desire to
praise your Holy name.
(2-17-2013)

DEALING WITH LIFE

I Often thought what
could have been, as I
traveled in this life.
Sometimes I'd question, why
there was so much strife.
Everyone wants to get ahead, but
get ahead where? No matter how much we get, we still are filled with care.
I want this, give me that, we struggle
everyday. We seek our person hood in
members of our clan. But, then again,
we don't go back where we all began. For we were **NOT** created
to be a person of sin. The first created were made with loving
peace within. But, once they sinned, then sin came in.
Oh, to be in a place sin does not abide,
To watch our friends and families truly walk side by side.
But at the close of each day, we still are filled with pride. We
want more, and more, and more, it can not be denied.
But things of earth will pass away, We are not guarantied another day.

For this life will come to an end,
Where will you spend eternity
my friend? Come to Christ and say,
Come into my heart and stay.
And let Jesus Christ
lead you all the way.
(1-14-2012)

**Jesus said, "He that hearth my word,
and and believeth on him that sent
me, hath everlasting life, and shall
not come into condemnation;
but is passed from death
unto life."
(John 5:24)**

TURN UP THE LIGHT

Light is available to all, so we might not fall.
Stand up tall, listen for God's call.
share your light as you walk along.
Soon others will join you in song.
Praise Him all ye people,
Shout it from the highest steeple.
Let your light burn bright and clear,
Declaring Jesus is so near.
Gracious by your word and deed
Then at the close of everyday,
You know that Jesus lead you all the way.
(Oct 21,2012)

THOUGHTS OF GOD

Safely I stand in the arms of the Lord,
Sheltered underneath His loving wings.
Knowing that He is the conquering King.
He is the Rock of ages for my soul.
(June 9, 2006)

ARE THEY READY?

Have we become complacent as we sit and warm a pew?
We need to look around for souls who need CHRIST too.
Don't lay this job on others who already have CHRIST'S view,
Because CHRIST gave you a commandment to love your neighbors too.
We need to be bold to those in need, share the GOSPEL, plant the seed.
For people in our life think every things okay,
They forget that at the end of life they will have to pay.
Heaven or hell where will they be?
Their destination depends on you and me
For GOD gave us a job to do,
Ask for GOD to keep you true.
For by HIS death HE paid the way it's true,
If we're bound for HEAVEN let's take others too.
JESUS came to seek the lost an if we belong to HIM we could,
Be about our FATHER'S business as in the LORD said we should.
10/15/13

HOW NOT TO START THE DAY

I jumped out of bed, and said
to myself, "it's a brand new day."
To get things done, and then to play.
But right away, things went so
wrong, and the day would drag on,
oh, so long.
Then I stopped and sat awhile,
and to my face there came a smile.
Then the Spirit spoke to me,
the best way to start the day,
It's with the Lord, and a time
to pray, Thank you Lord.
Remember, yes remember do,
and know that God's Word is true.
(10-21-2012)

COMFORT HE GIVES

I sat across the table
from a very empty chair
Just a few days ago.
You, my love, sat there.
Now grief fills my soul,
For we were the whole.
But, I must say goodbye for awhile.
I know God welcomed you home.
And someday very soon,
I will see you across the room.
For now, I serve and wait
Till King Jesus opens the glory gates.
"Written for those who have been
separated from their loved ones."
(1-10-2012)

TRAIN UP A CHILD

When we hold our little darlings in our arms at their birth,
Oh what joy we feel our hearts are filled with mirth.
To see their precious faces, count all their fingers and toes,
Run our hand across their tiny head and touch their tiny nose.
A baby is a precious gift one we need to train while small.
To listen an obey GOD'S word so when he or she is tall,
they can resist Satan's call.
If we make sure they know the LORD and walk with HIM each day,
though days may be hard, by CHRIST'S side they will stay.
10/12/13

DARE TO SHARE

Contented LORD to be with YOU and rest in YOU alone,
and one day soon I will see YOU seated upon YOUR throne.
With the sages from all ages we will shout and sing praising to YOU alone.
LORD as we await for that special hour,
Let us draw upon YOUR power.
To share with those who need YOU so ,
walking with darkness in their souls.
For each day for them remains the same,
May I share with others the reason YOU came.
You came into this world of sin,
to die for us and cleanse us within.
For GOD so loved the world it's true,
that's why HE died for me and you.
Ask the LORD to forgive your sins,
then invite HIM to come in.
Things will never be the same,
when you pray in JESUS' name.
10/14/13

"But ye shall receive power, after that the Holy Ghost is come upon you;
And ye shall be witnesses unto me both in Jerusalem, and in all Judeas,
And in Samaria, and unto the uttermost part of the earth."
(Acts 1:8).

MY DREAM OF HEAVEN

In my sleep I journeyed to a place so unfamiliar that I could
not understand how I could have gotten there.
The buildings were filled with clutter, but in a way the clutter was familiar
to me. Dates and times were written on objects just within my reach. As I
reached out to touch it, it would disappear leaving holes in certain areas.
Searching for answers, I went further into the building. There were dirty
look—ing bags tied at the top with beautiful red ribbons. I wondered
what could be inside. As I touched each one, they also disappeared.
I saw at the other end of the room a narrow stair case lighted brightly, and I
knew it went up. As I climbed upward, I seemed to feel lighter. This seemed
very strange indeed. Nevertheless, I continued upward. I could hear voices way
in the distant, but I could not make out any words that they were saying.
And I saw the faces of loved ones weeping over those who had departed.
I thought to myself, I need to leave this place of sadness.
I traveled on down the hallway, and I saw another sign on these doors:
ENTER WITH VICTORY AND REJOICING WITHIN.

As I pushed open the door, the scene was very different. People were crying, but not in defeat, but in joy for they knew that they would see their loved ones again in heaven.

What a contrast between these two sets of rooms!

The difference was HOPE!

I felt myself uplifted and renewed in my strength.

I was told that the bags that I had seen earlier were burdens of the saints, and the red ribbons represented the blood of our Lord Jesus Christ that sealed our burdens and took them away.

A song came into my mind that I had not remembered for years. I started to sing in my heart with new joy. "Will there be any stars, any stars in my crown, when at evening the sun goeth down, when I wake with the blest in that mansion of rest, will there be any stars in my crown."

Then I heard words in my heart and mind, **"Be at peace, your loved ones are comforted in my presence . Their journey is complete in Me. Their life of sorrow is past."**

HEAVEN HOME

FOR
Millions of Believers

Paul said, "For to me to live is Christ, and to die is gain.
For I am in a strait betwixt two, having a desire to depart,
and to be with Christ; which is far better."
(Phil. 1:21,23).
Jesus has saved believers, "To an inheritance incorruptible, and undefiled,
and that fadeth not away, reserved in heaven for you (them)." (I Peter 1:4).
"They shall see his face,–
There shall be no night –"
(Rev. 22).

JESUS IS THE WAY TO HEAVEN
Jesus said, "I am the way, the truth, and the life; no
man cometh unto the Father but by me."
(John 14:1-6). Jesus came down from heaven to die on the cross to pay for
your sins, and to take you to heaven. " — we have redemption through his
blood, the forgiveness of sins, according to the riches of his grace." (Eph.
1:7). Grace is Jesus's free gift of, "eternal redemption for us." (Heb. 9:12). We
cannot earn heaven, but Jesus paid for it, and we can receive it by faith.
Jesus gives eternal life to all who believe. " For God so loved the
world, that he gave his only begotten Son, that whosoever believeth in
him should not perish, but have everlasting life. "(John 3:16). Believe
you have sinned, and that Jesus can save you from your sins.
PRAY: JESUS, SAVE ME FROM MY SINS, AND TAKE ME TO HEAVEN: Jesus
says to you, "He (YOU) that **heareth** my word, and **believeth** on him that sent me

hath everlasting life, and shall not come into condemnation, **but is passed from death (hell) unto life (heaven)**. (John 5:24). Dear, Jesus, come into my heart, I believe you died for my sins, so that I can have everlasting life. I want to go to heaven. Dear Jesus, I believe you have saved me, help me to study the Bible, and to share it with others .

Then Jesus said, "I will use the lives of people who have left behind memories of their sorrows and pains, and their sufferings for Jesus. Their memories will touch the hearts of unbelievers. Some will come to believe in me because of the lives and the deaths of the faithful. Be faithful weary pilgrim the morning I can see, just take up your cross and follow close to Me." My awaking was a hard thing, during that short period of time the faces of loved ones flashed into my mind, and they didn't want to leave. I awoke with the thought, What Joy will come in the Morning! PRAISE BE TO GOD WHO IS OUR ALL AND IN ALL!

"Let not your heart be troubled; ye believe in God, believe also in me. In my Father's house are many mansions— I go to prepare a place for you. — I will come again, and receive you unto myself; — Jesus saith, I am the way, the truth, and the life, no man cometh unto the Father; but by me." (John 14;1-6).

Printed in the United States
By Bookmasters